EASY
COLORING BOOKS

FOR ADULT

PUBLISHED IN 2018 BY
KODOMO PUBLISHING

COPYRIGHT 'ILLUSTRATIONS' 2018 KODOMO PUBLISHING
ALL RIGHT RESERVED. 'NO PART OF THIS PUBLICATION MAY BE REPORDICED OR TRANSMITTED IN ANY
FORM OR BY ANY MEANS. ELECTRONIC, OR MECHANICAL,INCLUDING PHOTOCOPY, RECORDING OR ANY
INFORMATION STORAGE SYSTEM AND RETRIEVAL SYSTEM WITHOUT PERMISSION IN WRITING BY
PUBLISHER 'KODOMO PUBLISHING'

PRINTED IN THE UNITED STATES OF AMERICA

COLOR TEST PAGE

www.ingramcontent.com/pod-product-compliance
Lightning Source LLC
Chambersburg PA
CBHW062221220526
45471CB00009B/3302